Dedicated to the person I found hardest of all to love, but who I now love more deeply and unconditionally than I knew possible - Myself.

Copyright © Shirley Harvey 2016
All rights reserved. No part of this book may be reproduced, transmitted, or stored in an information retrieval system in any form or by any means, graphic, electronic, or mechanical, including photocopying, taping, and recording, without prior written permission from the publisher.

First edition 2016
ISBN 978-1-7750646-2-6

Published by Animal Publications in a magical place called Shirley World.
www.shirleyharvey.com

Written and illustrated by Shirley Harvey

It's never the right time to give up hope,
to lay down your dreams and sit and mope,
to give up on holding that open space
for the one that you love to take their place.

Good things come to those who wait;

a moment's pause is never too late.

Sometimes another needs more time

to come to you when all is fine.

patience

Why did the chicken cross the road?

Was it to kiss a handsome toad

or was it to sit on her favourite bench

or escape a truly unmentionable stench?

What ever it was, it was also a chance

for an act of kindness and maybe romance.

kindness

"We're polar opposites," said bear one day
to his bestest friend as they went on their way.
"You're flippin' grrrreat," he continued to speak,
"I love your waddle and your shiny beak."

"Well thank you," said penguin, all aglow
"You bring me joy, like a flurry of snow.
You make me feel happy on days when I'm grizzly,
I can bear-ly contain the joy that's within me."

When Debra the Zebra was super fine

with the way that her stripes did truly shine,

she discovered a really remarkable thing,

that she was so deeply loved by her king.

acceptance

It doesn't much matter if you come last or first,

if you arrive slowly or barge in with a burst.

What matters is celebrating the strengths that you've got

and celebrating that others have your have-nots.

"I could eat you up, I could, I could.

I would swallow you whole, I would, I would.

But there's something about you,

Something so sweet,

Something so innocent,

It makes my heart beat."

"I know," replied Mouse.

I offer you shelter,

I offer you refuge,

Here in my arms,

Away from the deluge.

I offer protection,

From below and above,

Because that's what you do

When you are in love.

protection

Open up wide,

let me look deep inside.

I want to observe

but I'm gonna need nerve.

It is scary for you

and for me too,

but I'm feeling brave

so don't misbehave.

There once was a frog who was sad,

all alone on a lily pad,

then one beautiful day

she opened his way

and her beauty did make his heart glad.

"Well I say, dear son,
Love just isn't fun
It's heartache and pain,
A most appalling game.
It leaves you sore,
It's worse than war.
Give it up for good,
You know you should."

"But that's not love,
all you said above.
It's rejection and loss
And fear and dross.
Love is patient and kind,
From the heart, not the mind.
Love is open and willing,
Overflowing, over-spilling.
Love is brave and strong,
Not weak and wrong.
So let go of your fear
And dive in with a cheer.

Courage

If I loved you as much as the moon loves the stars

And you loved me as much as Venus loves Mars,

Then it wouldn't much matter if the sky turned grey,

If I fell down a hole, or you lost your way,

Because we'd find our way, return to each other

As friends, as companions, as each other's lover.

together

be love.
x

Shirley is an artist, writer, entrepreneur and mother with a sweet and whimsical take on the world.

Using her unique style of painting and writing, and her team of trusted animal friends, she brings to light the finer qualities and quirks of what it means to be human with humour and grace.

www.shirleyharvey.com

www.ingramcontent.com/pod-product-compliance
Lightning Source LLC
LaVergne TN
LVHW071033070426
835507LV00003B/135